Song of the Republic

SAINT JULIAN PRESS

POETRY

Praise for SONG OF THE REPUBLIC

"McGrath's new book of poems shows him at one with nature in all its abundance and beauty, the earth, the heavens, and all the creatures, human beings included, that nature comprehends. The title of the collection, *Song of the Republic*, is reflected throughout, as is the threat to nature and to humanity, which is a condition of that republic."

    Richard F. Thomas, *George Martin Lane Professor of the Classics, Harvard University.*

SONG OF THE REPUBLIC

Kevin McGrath

SAINT JULIAN PRESS
HOUSTON

Published by
SAINT JULIAN PRESS, Inc.
2053 Cortlandt, Suite 200
Houston, Texas 77008

www.saintjulianpress.com

COPYRIGHT © 2020
TWO THOUSAND AND TWENTY
©KevinMcGrath

ISBN-13: 978-1-7330233-3-7
ISBN: 1-7330233-3-X

Library of Congress No: 2020943293

Cover Art Credit: 'Namibian Caryatid', courtesy of Kalulu, SA.
Author Photo Credit: Courtesy of Akos Szilvasi.

THE NAMES

Agatha ... 56
Amara ... 95
Angela ... 1
Anna ... 2
Antonia ... 20
Aria ... 4
Barbra ... 76
Beatricia ... 84
Camilla ... 53
Catalina ... 38
Celia ... 30
Cynthia ... 50
Debra ... 46
Diana ... 8
Domna ... 97
Dora ... 71
Elena ... 75
Ella ... 64
Emilia ... 31
Eva ... 67
Flavia ... 6
Gala ... 73
Gloria ... 43
Hana ... 45
Ilana ... 23
Isa ... 36
Juana ... 41

Julia ... 90
Karina ... 92
Laura ... 18
Leanora ... 37
Lilia ... 79
Lucia ... 58
Lydia ... 78
Lyra ... 48
Maria ... 3
Mona ... 69
Monica ... 28
Nina ... 83
Nora ... 16
Pia ... 62
Ramona ... 12
Sara ... 81
Serena ... 88
Sophia ... 35
Stella ... 14
Susanna ... 26
Sylvia ... 33
Tatiana ... 52
Thea ... 66
Tiara ... 10
Vana ... 39
Vita ... 86
Zora ... 99

FOREWORD

THE SONG OF THE REPUBLIC presents an ideal of consciousness that began on the Continent before the Europeans arrived with their exclusive Cartesian culture; this became the origin of our modern world and present Union. Here in the feminine voice of certain women is a narrative of that gathering of natural and impersonal awareness. This book presents an ideal of consciousness that existed in preliterate and premonetary northern America before the foreigners arrived with their newly printed and aniconic culture.

As migrants or fugitives we continually and perpetually cross the currents and oceans in order to achieve further universal liberty, as we struggle toward a scene that is out of time and whose reception qualifies our moral dignity and where a matchless solitude is our state; yet a solitude that is thoroughly and fully inclusive. This is the work of *poetry* as the sign moves among the lions, hounds, seabirds, and all of Adam's nominal creation. When we speak of freedom what we are actually telling of is our liberty to pursue a personal act of love without constraint.

Those who have nothing have the most to give and those without any place in life possess all of time, for the clarity of love supplies us with one just autonomy and then it is *that* which is ultimately true and without ethical deficiency. In so much necessary fabrication our small passing universe is then made strong.

'So why have you sent us into this world to be so alone and for so long and, how much must we endure and suffer in order to comprehend your beauty?' These are the questions American humanity repeatedly posed in its effort to assess and profound our manifest existence here. In the art of fiction, in the act of writing, in the pursuit of the genius of poetry and the concomitant extent of metaphor, we come close to a moral truth, more than in any other experience or worldly intimacy; for art is not life.

The metaphorical and immortal raptor—that totemic and emblematic bird whose aim is true—is pre-social, pre-discursive, and absolutely shaped. It is solely indicative as it flutters behind our eyelids and trembles upon our barely open lips and infinitely restless when we are witnessing and looking upon its rare and near-imperceptible profile, when we encounter that ruthless vision. If the prescient world of poetry precedes all duration and temporal exposition and any fashion of human volition is simply where an object is perceived as distinct from human consciousness and is therefore so desired, then in this unique art of invention there is transparency and sureness, lucidity that is perfectly still.

We are strangely obliged in our letters to admit a purely indestructible and irresistible right so that our tangible substance might endure and be tried, as we stand changeless and motionless in this severe yet wonderful New England terrain. These letters and names are what were ideally exchanged when those principal Americans gave title to all of life and its variety of marital being; they are the coins of our native goodness and all that is worthy in the natural world, where each day—just like a beautiful falcon—we work further towards a new order of comprehension and meaning, a streamlining of altruism which creates veracity within a given second.

From this point of view the action of love is our most profound and ineradicable condition in this world and our only true state of freedom; for love can cross an ocean in a few seconds—just like a hawk—and when we die all that remains is life. To take this point one step further: if consciousness is apart from the sensible world then the experience of consciousness is true, depicted here as a portrait of original land.

To Xanthe-Hero

Nel ciel che più de la sua luce prende
fu'io, e vidi cose che ridire
né sa né può chi di là sù discende …

Paradiso I,4-6

~ Song Of The Republic ~

ANGELA

I Like to watch you walk
And count the rings I never see
Yet how unbearable it is
Not giving to the one we love

Deft visceral autonomous gifts
Of time as years dilate
In my despair I visit paradise
None of the birds notice me

Swan geese heron gull
Their world is out of time
Desperation drove me there
Beyond the present circles

I was pleased not to exist
They did not see my soul
Pleased to vanish in this way
Disappearing inside heaven

Only love draws us back
When we are only giving
I love to watch you moving
Especially when you are alone

ANNA

The end that is always to come
But is only anticipated
Where does destiny begin
In what day or moment

Or in a well-loved promise
Is it fulfilled so simply
Does the presence of the wind
Affect living sentience

Fragrance of a human body
Enigma of human beauty
What is it we do not have
Which is so dispossessing

Being drawn by the not-having
And then in the satisfaction
We still miss the conclusion
To this long endless call

MARIA

There are two windows in this life
Through which quiet observers stare
One looks to the moral universe
And its immutable sky

The other turns within to where
Lovers meet in brief white fire
Becoming an insensible one
Where they might lose themselves

Between these transparent panes
Truth like flirtation passes
Involving eyes and hearts and
Hands that long to touch forever

Some in darkness live and grieve
Desperate for a single view
Of justice in reflection where
All that came before occurred

ARIA

I STOOD there once with you
A thousand years ago
Looking out onto the plain
From that vast archway

I knew then that time
Had graciously paused for us
Supplying those few minutes
With life imperishable

When you and I are gone
Those moments will not expire
For within that great door
So much was joined out of time

Even when the gateway and
Its stone platform collapse
We shall remain standing there
Between so many worlds

We only act once in life
In kind and how we move
Yet only when we love
Are we free and infinite

We cover ourselves in pure cloth
Perfecting a torso received
Yet the impersonal remains
Untouched by our casual ways

Love only occurs once
Endlessly renewed by the sun
As perpetually unbound we
Pretend to be conspiratorial

~ Song Of The Republic ~

Then far within the heart's core
Barely visible or conscious
The universe fits flawlessly
As we dress and undress -

The unbreakable inward harmony
Lens or tissue through which
We stare at this complete union
Of confusion and satisfaction

Caught in a net of birdsong
Of souls hidden within eyes
In those few seconds we share
All submission and surrender

FLAVIA

In the slow grey hour before dawn
We are momentarily unbound
Devising life and its heart
As if a prince of lightness

Like a groom before a bride
In the suddenness of passion
When humility makes us vulnerable
As the season is disclosed

For woman's love for man and
Man's love for woman are
Random not symmetrical
Profoundly out of time

Sometimes in the night we hear
Geese passing overhead
Returning to their ancient lakes
Which only they apprehend

Or like the beauty of a deer
Who walks among the trees
Crossing open fields when
No one in the world perceives

So too my love for you
As you stand naked and apart
Not apparent in this world
Just approached by acts of love

~ Song Of The Republic ~

The slight partition of the stars
That obscurity reveals as
Your guardians whose agency
And discretion lead our lives

You only exist in our eyes
We might never touch your body
You only repeat never conceive
As amorous you are made

To know of fortune is to trust
Faithful to your loveliness
Like a midnight river running
When the moon hides in cloud

DIANA

Stay hawk - there is no descent
There is only one day ever
In our lives and one occasion
For vision to be complete

Be unlike a dagger falling
Cutting the sacrificed year
Separating yellow light
From noon and zenith

Stay and do not stoop
Keep to what you see
Something permanent and
Beautiful without bitterness

Make no descent with
Red blades slanting and
Without a cry reveal
Voices hidden in the wheat

True places do not occur
Except in your heart
Among fresh leaves oscillating
Or footsteps receding from life

Glide away into grey air
Without wheeling and keep
Your horizon from igneous
Ancient unbearable grief

Stay high on summer and flower
Be the genius of birds
Proclaiming our promise
True sky and true curving stars

~ SONG OF THE REPUBLIC ~

Stay and never incline
To our one small day and night
Be among the circling hours
Our sharply human axle burning

TIARA

Now the sacred geese advance
In varying line southward
Across the coast and isles
The rocks tides currents sand

As crimson leaves descend so
The birds depart this world
Rivers cool and life sleeps
In a quiet onset of darkness

What mariners now put out
With small wooden sailing vessels
Going toward an horizon where
Solitude and emptiness are all

Humming-birds heron swans
Vanish into a lowering sky
As the air becomes cold and
All earthly light diminishes

A candid moon moves to circle
As dry hills become unstable
Grass and reeds fall down now
In this vast soundless demise

So many rings of shadow
That dance above our sleep
It is as if we are initiates
Into a secret of renewal

Hammers of wisdom in the heart
Formless and without dimension
Drive us toward one truth
Both weightless and transparent

~ Song Of The Republic ~

There a bitter fox resides
Snarling as the birds pass by
Raging at such departure and
The warmth still in their eyes

RAMONA

Under Polaris darkness spins
Rotates so invisibly
We cannot see this movement yet
Our constancy is perpetually moved

A golden rain of carnal joy
The silent pressure of the stars
Commit us to live in time
As days are circled round by years

The stiff knuckles of a hawk
Reddened by the blood of winter
Its beak raw and sharp with
Fragments of hardened snow

The bird surveys mortality
From soundless frozen air
No cry nor voice is ever heard
In this defeat of animal warmth

Like a meteor it falls down
Or like a comet's wake
The bird having sighted life
Strikes – exchanging souls

Midwinter as a grey sun pauses
Hovering above white distance
The hungry raptor oversees
This low motionless terrain

Winter with its rain and ice
Small dense uncoloured days
How we promise to be true
As we struggle on the plain

~ Song Of The Republic ~

The thin bare wind of winter
Sterile and unnourished
Blows across bones and hills
Without residence on earth

Fields are now transfixed by frost
Where slight footprints pass
Telling of their solitude
And of mute desperation

This is no worldly triumph
For only sleep is possible
Consciously the sky flares
At night beneath the hunting stars

Years like leaves are threshed
Shaken by the wind
Beneath a milky zenith and
Profane scabbard of life

Under Polaris light stays
Poised faithful and firm
We break our hearts with pathos
Yet fidelity is possible on earth

For there is victory even
In the weightless bird we glimpsed
In our words and affection
Giving ourselves away

STELLA

Tonight as a dead wind blows
And the dark lakes crack and
The unseen black river stiffens
I wish that you were in my arms

I wish that you came to my bed
And with kindness offered
Your admiration and with you
Without conscience I slept

If I called you here now
Would you approach and lightly
We could be perfectly without
Pretence or any disturbance

If you were in my arms now
Our understanding of the world
Might vanish in mutual symmetry
Leaving us simply believing

Yet the adverse wind blows
These slow hours are insufficient
For you sleep far away content
Unaware of how life could rest

Bare trees creak and scrape
No one bird nor small animal
Survives the absolute cold
Only love continues burning

So I summon you now
Pretending to say your name
When this emptiness resounds
Making quietness so impersonal

~ Song Of The Republic ~

For your heart is not beneath
My warm hand and no one
Is afoot on earth tonight
Except for solitary darkness

NORA

The luminous paramour who has no body
No name and speaks no word and knows
How it is to be human circling us
When we are still quiet in the world

Morning like an unseen raptor
With its hard blade of shadow
Falls on our deficient minutes
And our wounds of indecision

Then the flames surround us
Clear lucid invisible fire
As each quick day vanishes
In haste as if hunted by hawks

In this seasonal flamboyance
We are stripped of all clothing
Ingenious hands barely touch
Blameless and sincere

Superhuman are those hours
With eyes gently closing
They judge us for our kindness
Our attention to their light

Exhilaration runs on the air
Knowing there is only innocence
Cruel and separating lovers
Shining severely as they embrace

Beneath a heavenly universe
Stars pause each vivid second
Their secrecy of truth is just
A friend with whom we walk

~ Song Of The Republic ~

Miraculous like nothing on earth
This companion who takes us away
With the moral beauty of courtship
Deluding us of absence

For supernatural is this life
Unspeakably loyal and so inviting
Regardless of how we pretend
We are here for ever

All creation now observes
This secret of true love
We enter the world but are prior to life
As sunlight enters each following day

LAURA

Beside a grey-green lake
Beneath a livid sunless sky
You and I walked once
Recalling our years together

Within the surrounding forest
So many lives were watching
Staring at us speechless
Admiring our old friendship

As the powder in a shell
Knows nothing of the world
So we in our affection
Ignored so much life

Snow has now silenced
The water and the trees
Deadened all the roads
Hiding every footstep

Without amity in life
We cannot exist and yet
If we do not admit
To human suffering we fail

The desire to end desire
Is not desire but passion
Indifferent to ideals and
Refusal to be faithless

Light intercepted by
The beauty of a living body
So we become aware
How shadow changes shape

~ Song Of The Republic ~

All night the twanging ice
All day a birdless blue air
Water beneath the surface
So still as to be eternal

Grey ice in thick plates
Broken and dispersed onshore
How we built a column of pieces
An infinite pillar we adored

On the lake a shell breaks
No one hears a sound
So in our humanity
We betray all admission
Our hope the dust of stars

ANTONIA

All victory can be broken
By the great extent of solitude
Loneliness will crush happiness
Leaving mastery alone

The sun our only vessel can
Founder upon despair
Both personal and universal
Random captious haste

My ancestral man who
Has walked ten thousand years
Who simply stands and waits
Regardless of time going

Observing us but unaware
That we are his far-children
Spawned by his old lust or
What became a slow loving

Tired of only weeping in
This watery acumen of days
How is it we are separate
When we are in fact the same

Stone copper wood bones
Which first gave you music
Flutes and songs remade
From the shoulder of a bird

There is no earthly purchase
But a long courageous going
From life to life in circles
Where the sun sings its journey

~ Song Of The Republic ~

A beautiful sleek torso
Of a creature lost in shadow
The eternal object of a song
With its own sufficient instant

Sunlight proclaims our destiny
Omits the moral darkness
The uncommon and so evasive
World where we are confined

Girls among the green wheat
Young men lying by a river
All the animate world is so
Determined by this symmetry

No bird crosses the cold air
No fish moves beneath the ice
No voice happiness nor expression
Comes between sky and ground

Throwing stones on frozen water
Watching waiting for a sign
To reveal itself and dart amongst
The dull brown unprinted forest

Vulnerable and so fragile
We walk ten thousand centuries
The lakes remain and the rocks
There is no mortal treasure

Yet trees are dressed in light
Young animals upon their boughs
And gifts of truth are hidden
In slight acts of compassion

~ SONG OF THE REPUBLIC ~

We must believe our goodness
For that is all our time is worth
Let us renew our promise so
Kindness treads a flat terrain

~ Song Of The Republic ~

ILANA

Fragrance of low evening sky
Brazen sunlight glancing down
Breathless owls glide toward
A cold and lifeless forest

Beauty of a nude figure
Walking on deserted land
A true man and true wife
Joined by abounding nature

We cannot dismiss the world
Because it is not solemn
For the universe does not
Accept a moral force in life

There is no judgement
Inhabiting an austere sky
When the lions stand about
Waiting for us to speak

For the envelopes they bring
To be simply opened and
Thousands of many years
Will vanish in that second

As we walked upon a frozen lake
Grey air fog and creaking
Where the waters began to split
And gelid leaves decay -

I told the sea beneath our feet
A secret we had kept
As long as youth and beauty last
We are caught by a thread

~ Song Of The Republic ~

I told our secret to the sea
To the grass and fields of sand
How days are not days upon
The tense membrane of time

Into a shimmering darkness
Running with music and light
I told the ancient coastal air
Of what we could not say

Beneath the powdered stars
Only the soul is real
A small luminous circle
Suspended between sky and water

This is a perfect work
Above all that is
The mower with stone and blade
Who never desists from labour

If the spirit is alive then
A lost soul is a ghost
Phosphoros speeding in the night
A heart driving toward its mate

How can we match time
With so much uncertainty
Indelible and lucid passion
Set in a world of cavities

I know my love for you
Is less than your worth
But I long for that moment
When our desire is equal

~ Song Of The Republic ~

Paradox or dilemma
Like water we may not drink
Yet my thirst is not fluid
Just as the stars do not speak

I know my love for you
As a light that moves always
Towards the shade and yet
We never touch nor stay

So much new water
Running through our blood
Renewing life's motive
Always transporting us

Fluctuation of the river
Its eyeless sweeping heaven
A sun that never pauses
As if sleeping on the wing

Then your hands reach down
Entering the heart
A place no one mentions
Where we were once founded

Now as I take myself
To the room where you reside
Where I say your name
May my words be acceptable
As grain hidden in the wheat

SUSANNA

GEESE circling in wide arcs
Above a frozen lake
As evening reclines upon
Grasses and brown reed

Beside this crimson water
Trees are black and aged
As shadows rise upward
Toward the gathering birds

Frost snow ice mist
Hail wind and thunder
The fluency of the sky
Moves like a slow broad river

We walk on earth a brief while
Accomplishing our words
Ascending and descending
As if a strange rare speech

Like years these archaic birds
Come and go and re-appear
With their streaming speech
Dissolve mundane experience

I have seen the geese gather
Upon the stiff dry earth
Dark wings resting upon rushes
Beside the river in early spring

In rain fugitive from wind
The air noisy and disturbed
I have heard them closely singing
Unsheathed - stripped of frailty

~ Song Of The Republic ~

Calling all the universe
With commonplace humility
Their solemn careful sound
Is witness of no aspiration

Such music is unspeakable
Becoming distant and unheard
Despite our indecency and
Dilemmas of enduring grief

This vision of acoustic life
As a cold river runs coastward
And magnolia forsythia crocus
Colour small resolute days

Inevitable and unfamiliar
Infinitely continuous
Between diaphragm and heart
All the world is going

There are no leaves upon the trees
No courtship nor contest of life
No blood exposed nor incited
Being far removed from this hour

As the year dies and then reforms
Crossing between time and light
In the temperament of their song
We forget anguish or ambition

Friction of language and dust
Where so much is crucified each day
In the beauty of the birds' singing
Suffering does not compromise -
We benefit from their praise

MONICA

Who are you lying there
Asleep on the snow
So invincible once
King or queen of the air

Crimson bronze yet cold
Now stiff with ice and stone
Your heart remains perpetual
Gentle warm and fierce

The hiding of your mastery
Was the origin of our life
How you never suffered nor
Accepted earthly distress

How can mystery perish
What journey out of time
Is this that you have made
Descending from endless height

Once you held a mirror
Deep within your eyes
Looking down upon the universe
On every moving kind

A scabbard of affection
Whose fame is made of light
You oversaw our lives as
The wind caressed your body

Always innocent you were
Your beauty had no sheath
Like heaven at night gazing
Observing our progress

~ Song Of The Republic ~

Sovereign beauty of the world
Without heart or repetition
Without days nights or years
You are infinitely enduring

Always present in the distance
Observing us with compassion
You are the only one and
So we adore your ways

In the slim fissure between
Sea and reddening sky
Your body is revealed to us
And then time is transformed

There is no horizon now
As fiery dancers undulate
On a cold grey-blue ocean
Where we begin and end

Your face streams with spray
There is no grief only
The play and dive of white birds
Who escort you for ever

Those immutable forms
Of shadows on the land
Offer us our single freedom
To apprehend your bounds

Before kings and queens
All this had been foretold
There is no deception now
During swift footed darkness

CELIA

If memory unbecomes us
For submitting to no rule
We seek to emulate that way
By offering our desire

Footprints drying in the air
That approach and vanish
Perfume of lime trees that
Fills the night with volume

Foot-marks upon the earth
Where once a being passed
Haunting us with a shape
Not to be transformed

Where will they lead us to
And might we then return
If the experience is more
Than human vanity allows

EMILIA

Like a swallow you were
Precise in your kindness
Quick as you flew away
Into colourless morning

How the human spirit
Glides apart from the body
Soundless even without breath
Becoming absolute once more

Will the swallow find a house
In the ashes of a human soul
As a voice rises toward the sun
Saying - we are perfectly alone

Through the cracks of every rock
Where iris and crocus unfold
Beneath smooth wings of time
You shall make a new dwelling

In fragility honesty quietness
Poised in private devotion
Careful toward humanity
Who know nothing at all

Yet treasuring all modesty
Lucid as a flawless vessel
The integrity of a thousand years
Turned from a potter's hand

We each possess two destinies
In this world and beyond
And what we accomplish here
Attends us in the future

~ Song Of The Republic ~

The beauty horror and the pity
As we go from room to room
Certain of immortality yet
Unsure of how it is we lived

If we could count our bones
What would they tell us
Of the vision we express
As we go so mysteriously

Where shall swallows settle
This spring as they dash north
In possession of no doubt
Keeping only to the light

Their honesty is that we see them
And sometimes hear a word
Even as they cross darkness
In complete silence saying -

We are perfectly alone and
That is our earthly joy
This is how true lovers give
Their promise back to life
Graciously returning

~ Song Of The Republic ~

SYLVIA

So many spirits in the air
Like grassy rainfall or the sonorous
Unseen voice of slender birds
Among trees leafing to the light
As finely luminous days encircle
Us with slim mysterious bodies
Where happiness is to forget
The casual dust at our feet
And stripped of living thought
We are held within this vision
To conceive of how to love
By nakedness impressed
Upon this old and fluvial coast
Where candid life is now sustained

Time witnesses each second
How all being can possess
A small portion of the future
For tomorrow only drives us
Onward making us forget
Blood streaming on a dawn sky
The green running of a current
Fluid air that we consume
Causing breath to speak
Now the universe involves us
Stays on our tongue and in
The subtle movement of our eyes
Impersonal without right
Is the virtue of our release

Like a lioness in apple blossom
Now that the rains have come
As all threads run with light
Earth drinks entirely of love
Seed and fruit gently unite

~ Song Of The Republic ~

Free at last of worldly time
In a vault of the flaming
Life is not restrained
So our stamina is refreshed
Loosed of shadowy passion as
The lioness cries out aloud
And apple blossom collapses
When we pursue an inward light
Admitting to moral truth

Now the year wears antlers
As it walks beneath the dawn
Risen from the tomb of winter
Where seeds were kept hidden
Now both hare and deer
Step from the forest edge
On gracious fields wandering
Beside increasing lakes
So you and I are wakened
By so much vivid beauty
Until one solitary evening
As we stroll about the saplings
This mutual life draws us away
Going beyond all happiness

SOPHIA

I DECK the house in flowers
A wreath for the door
A vase of barley for the table
Beside the bed some tissue poppies
Of the most intense of madder

Vine leaves for the chimney
Anemone for window jambs
One could continue so for ever
The gate - steps to the path
But there are ends

A garland for a roof post
And time will marry time
This ring which one makes - saying
This is where you are and were
And this was simply happy
Shared by those who form your thought

Remember - the rest is not
Possible to ever hold
Is impossible to covet
The colours go but not the point

ISA

She files her nails with the grace of a wren
Till they shine like a polished willow grove
And whilst she works her fingertips fine
He plays for her on his bamboo flute

Her eyes are as pure as the pearl skin of shells
Her limbs are like feathers adrift in the sea
For the joy of her beauty and flight of her voice
He plays to her on his bamboo flute

Her feet are unslippered and dance through the tide
Her dance for the moon is covered with leaves
As lightly she steps through sonorous waves
To the tuning of his bamboo flute

LEANORA

Here they are panting teeth bared
With hazy eyes and slow steps
Bright red dogs without any sky
As the hills turn into powder

With a hiss of insects at noon and
Liquid torches of fireflies at night
On the river a slow green mist
Hangs opaque with humid odour

Dawns are turbid and smoulder
Flicker through dense foliage
Days wheel by with dull tension
As the dogs growl in the distance

The year hovers balanced
Guarded on either side
The tongue of the beast flashes
Light held tightly between iron paws

Soon the hounds will slowly
Be pacing home in the dusk
Along the terraces distributing
Their gold in the low red light

Are we vulnerable now - deceived
Without origin or possible fiction
The scarlet dogs hold up a mirror
Where our supposed unity vanishes

Hot fiery snarling with joy
The vermilion dogs of summer
The sky fuses in a blur of lead
And shadows snap at their edges

CATALINA

If the pursuit of happiness
Portrays how it is that we
Apprehend the stillness of life
Not empty but perpetual

Now at this haying time
As a tall sun hovers
And a world gently pauses
Consumed by powdery heat

Beneath a low shadow of cedar
Upon warm grey rocks
A girl and a boy say what
No one else on earth knows

Across the grass - under the leaves
As quick swallows perforate
Soft opaline dusty air
One word secures our pursuit

Despite the snarling cruelty
That inhabits so much time
Like a snake defining its grief
Or the walls we must overcome -

All our efforts to succeed
Cannot speak of what it is
That we harvest from our days
Beyond the captivation of love

VANA

In these furtive new days
I walked out towards a lake
A thin quiet rain was falling
Upon the still grey water

Circumambulating the margin
I swam for a long hour
Then followed a curving river
Drifting gently onto the coast

I found a boat beside the shore
And embarked upon the sea
The purpose of the universe
Was there upon those waves

So we begin another world
Never sleeping never waking
Crossing from season to season
In the recession of the year

If all sentiment is only received
When do we begin to forget
For without recollection
There can be no amity

What spiritual innovation
Is sovereign at this time
If causality is delivered
To us rather than practiced

Love truth the beautiful
Were there upon the horizon
Consciousness became untimely
As shadows prepared to depart

~ Song Of The Republic ~

Just like sudden diamonds
Trees constantly aflame
Or like the red morning
That comes to us each day

Within the dawn we always meet
Beneath the noon embrace
Then in subtle evening
There is no drowning in the waves

At this cadence I began
Living from minute to minute
For there was no more promise
In the spontaneous light

JUANA

The first yellow ribbons unfurl
Of witch-hazel and forsythia
As purple croci arise
And the sacrificial hyacinth

Heron and young swan descend
And iridescent swallows
Return from the heated south
As nightingales declaim dawn

Revived and absolved from winter
All that solitary grief and
Loneliness of sunless skies
Despair of being without love

This ingenious multitude of life
Appears to sing and dance
Orchestra of impassioned colour
Of courtship and brooding geese

Eyebrows of the year move
As the goat whose throat we cut
Is spitted upon coals - devoured
Mixed and consumed with wine

Bronze hawks and glossy ravens
Who kill for pleasure and blood
Stain our vernal altars
With the ruins of their feast

Upon the river narrow boats
Set off for summer rituals
Running down toward the coast
Driven by boundless admission

~ Song Of The Republic ~

Once again we are encircled
Drawn back to the old dance
Where footsteps and music measure
How it is that bodies join

A man and woman have come
Out of us into the world
Entering upon this vision
Of the reduplicating year

Magnolia and almond blossom
And the virgin dogwood
Offer their nuptial beauty now
To this miraculous promise

GLORIA

How is it two people love
What is it they see
When in their silent prowling
They meet irresistibly as if
Ingenuous in matrimony
Like water as it touches grain
Or intimation of what drives
A man and woman to surrender
To the perfume of their nakedness
As in connubial light they are
Revealed and stripped bare of all
But their nature and its touch
So they might slightly witness
The genius of beauty hidden

There are swimmers in the sun
Or birds in a palace of wind
Who mirror perfectly desire
Making love transparent
Weightless and without cause
Becoming the first landscape
Rich with amorous passion
Their skins stained with saffron
Of both desire and death until
They disclose their liquid heart
Diminishing all suffering
Making this completely beautiful
Phenomenal and virtuous
Not mistaking dawn for noon

How long is a day if
It be hidden without light
Refulgent and attractive
Without scent of human breath
That immutable agency

~ Song Of The Republic ~

When the loss of our perfection
Is more distressing than
Spiritual beauty vanishing
Just as a boy and girl attract
Each other and dominate the earth
Proclaiming thoughtlessness
Then launching into night
A vessel and casting thin sails
Where the wind can lean and press

Iridescent now is solitude
As the year hovers above zenith
When wanton light lives alone
Craving the company of darkness
Then lovers hold in their arms
All they might ever confess
For wheels are always circling
Never knowing of just release
That perfect man and woman
Who conceived the future twice
Mysterious and inseparable
They were consumed unbearably
Their solitude lightly unmade
As intimacy became discretion

HANA

Where is the messenger we wanted
Already a brief season declines
We stood on the shore paraded
Roads and avenues and called
Yet no one answered us

The stiff blue silk of summer
Imprinted with courting birds
Has become limp and colourless
An unalterable sky is lightless as
Space and time re-enter the heart

An age of heroes has gone to dust
Gone are the unavailable women
There was no messenger - fooled
We should have enjoyed ourselves
We called only to prove a reason

We thought we were captive
Not fugitive - marked
An illusory world of play
Dust has become so heavy now
A few grains keep us from going

DEBRA

WHAT sleeps in us sleeps
In all the world and
With one intimacy
Even suffering is enjoined
Upon our tongues

Yet on either side of sleep
Consciousness stays awake
In life and death and
The world we have lost

Our one triumph is
We find victory in our loss
Securing from the beautiful
From so much ephemera
Making light the weightless

There is no centre to love
Not even for lovers beside
Each other quietly
Deeply naked with oblivion

We are only what we receive
Neither more nor less
For there are two rooms in life
And our body the threshold
Current in a profound sea

Where a door made of lust
Of flesh and of desire
And warm human blood
Stays open all the days

~ Song Of The Republic ~

Like the pure white lions
Whose thin red lips await
This beauty that is out of time
Cannot be perceived
Except the perfume of its breath

As shadows on a dry plain
Cast down upon the world
From clouds going above
Our ways move perpetually
Even beneath our eyelids

Their satisfaction is so brief
Yet more than compelling
Toward luminous endurance
One or two make a way

Invisibly we are hidden
By all our craving
Covered as if with cloth
In which our gorgeous
Nakedness is displayed

The ellipsis lovers make
Visceral ribbon of life
Their pendulum of loving
Cyanine with new blood

One just tensile strength
Simply bends and releases
And even grief and joy
In time must desist
True to what we do not know

LYRA

One day perhaps you will recall
A young man who pursued you
Who took you to the pine-tree hills
Down to a bay on the other coast

The salt water where we swam
The gentle groves where we slept
Were you never tempted to
Surrender what you did not know

As people who live in boats
Or bees and cicadas among leaves
Are always wakeful to the air
The movement of the wind

Your beauty drew the eyes of many
As did your light and agile voice
You were so many women then
So many wished to follow you

The sound of horses in the night
Hooves upon polished stone
Was not that like time itself
Passing unseen beyond you

What did you gather in your arms
Or make of those nights
Gifts received and not conveyed
Back toward the hands of life

Are you absent from the sun
Now that your hair is grey
Did your beauty like an arrow
Find a heart in which to rest

~ Song Of The Republic ~

Now as you walk your city ways
Among sparrows in the orange trees
Beneath the palms you might recall
Who made words in your name

CYNTHIA

PHENOMENAL and most beautiful
You are the one life here
That watched us for millennia
Wolf coyote fox in likeness
Who guards the fires and camps
Abandoned long ago when ice
Vanished from the entire land
Seeped into the underworld
As grey as a thin shade you
Go shuttering among the trees
Are present just in passing
Both motionless and subtle
Dressed in abstract black you tread
Unaware of us yet mourning

When once we lay with you
That was the beginning
Of compassion in the world
Unknowing of your own life
Unwitnessed even by yourself
You now walk the barest roads
Never making any journey
Your shadow has detached
From its formal living body
Thoughtless of us and gentle
Our source of worldly amity
Yet the origin of remorse
Core of singular despair
Your contempt made us strong

Your cruelty purified experience
How you stared made us move
As when beside a woman man
First rested in the universe
Careless of our dryness now

~ Song Of The Republic ~

Beneath the summer trees
Yet being so fulfilled you are
Always about to depart
When miracles are fugitive
And moonlight fills the world
In sheets of undressed monochrome
You go on naked planes of light
Patterning the virtuous stars
Where our ambition is converted

Now with you we enter time
You brightest being of the night
Yet love will always disappear
Like rain that offers carnal life
Or seeds unwinding in the dark
Hunting for their first impulse
Or squalls of thunder striking
Onto an arid ground
When inspiration is discarded
Once breath begins to speak
You then elect us to suffer
So in the end we can see
Offering rare and lovely truth
Making light of our need

TATIANA

Geese landing upon a lake
In the final red bars of dusk
The soft noise of a hundred wings
Mowing through cool dark air

From over smooth hills they came
Crying out in long formation
Above a half-moon was gaping
At a brilliant white planet

Onto calm water descending
Something greater than we ever were
Rising and falling onto a lake
Circling low in black emptiness

Further off in a house children
Were imitating a tune
As the last thin pink rays went
From a primitive sky to another world

Reversal of so much human life
We repeat thinking we invent
Sleep fills our hemisphere as
An owl glides from its wood

~ Song Of The Republic ~

CAMILLA

A LION walks in the shade
The vine curls about a stem
The sun is stronger and brighter
Although the hours diminish

Evening will come soon as
A mower advances through light
A lilac-hyacinth sky is tinted
With subtle strands of pink

Broad long fields are being hayed
The air sweet with seeds and dust
Calmness as low shadows rest
All being presently still

A fawn is solitary in the woods
Fern and birch are wet from night
There is a sound of falling water
For hours from eaves to earth

There is a gentle passive murmur
Of rain upon slow waves
The ancestors have all departed
Gone up to the far mountains

They stare down at us in silence
At dusk as long days recede
Listening to streams running
A grey sound upon cold cedars

Pine-needles pollen feathers
Stones gather upon the floor
Spiders weave in the threshold
Wooden rooms are empty of time

~ Song Of The Republic ~

Goodness and children and dogs
Small animals that inhabit this world
This low venerable isle of rock
All pause in strict lightness

On this finest day to heaven
Thank you dear friend for
The voice that you once gave us
Without which nothing exists

Like a bird flying at night
Soundless through dark air
All that life transfigures
Lacks recognition without amity

The lion walks in shadow
The hours though more intense
Rich with fullness are smaller
Diminished in their amplitude

Each cool damp dawn as
We walk beside this still blue lake
When leaves are fresh upon
Dust of a white limestone track -

No matter how much we suffer
Whatever ordeal and agony
By going just one second further
One fraction of an instant ahead -

Our vision will always succeed
Finding goodness in truth
So thank you for your bond
Your kindness and affection

~ Song Of The Republic ~

Thank you for this world
For your companionship and
Happy places where we walked
For only you have made us love

The stillness of the house now
Of life and of hills and lake
Of geese cormorant sails and skies
As swallows thread the air
The harvest is taken in and stored

AGATHA

On my sixty-sixth year on earth
I walked out for distraction
Loving the sand loving the dust
The unmasking of the air

A firm wind from off the lake
Was bevel on the hot light
As if desperate for release
For destiny to be complete

The distances were hazy and
The low brown hills at rest
As my years gathered close
Awaiting their dismissal

So much time so little place
So little achieved in living
Yet this is where my heart stays
Where I wish to sleep

Unknown unseen yet observant
Printless on this soft ground
No one on earth knows
How we are here nor why

The low green water of the lake
Where heron stood composed
Was perfect in its stillness
Untroubled by humanity

The dry flat plain extended
For invisible miles away
As among the thorns I walked
And at each step vanished

~ Song Of The Republic ~

All of moral life and vision
Ordeals of simple human effort
Were less than this beauty
Without grief only promise

There was no oblivion here
And yet no awareness
A terrain of stone and powder
Of old mineral detritus

For one grain of consciousness
Is more victorious than any joy
This strong light-blue light
Luminous draws us elsewhere

Perfectly stationary as we wander
It supports all we know
Yet our feet do not touch
Its worldly genius of love

On my sixty-sixth year of time
Obedient to perpetuity
With hawks and lapwings
With the speed of kingfishers
In the light of truth there is no one

LUCIA

THESE slow and towering days
As summer loses its head
Fields of dusty bronze grain
Stiffen in powdery air
Carnal bodies and naked feet
Move careless into the future
Where the mystery of volition
Is driven to confess its doubt
Attrition in the human soul
Phosphorescence of quiet suffering
Now solitude buries its heart
Within unspeakable grief
In this enigma of loneliness
When truth is being expressed

If affliction is our source
Vision going beyond ordeal
What can we believe or
Insist upon when only nil
Surrounds us with its cycles
If we are unbearably free
And liberty stays the ground
Apprehending fidelity that
Place where we might love
Why are we still enslaved
As all receipts like ancient rain
Only sustain one vivid need
For consciousness to retouch life
With fragile efforts of conception

Through a porthole the sea
Is always breaking beside us
Green timely and evasive
Driven by a struggling wind
Whilst on deck the crew

~ Song Of The Republic ~

Prepare the burial of a companion
Pilot who once guided us
Through years of desperation
They stitch the canvas and weigh
The body with old red iron
Leaving it to sink astern
Vanishing with foam and anguish
Now there is no cause to weep
Only indifference and isolation

So here we pose and vanish
Disappear without affection
Having given and receded
Drawn out onto the waves
As pity and grief sink down
Leaving a few empty shells
Where we slowly mourn
For all of our existence
Then it is we might perceive
Treasuries of unearthly kind
Bow before those guardians
Who creep from the soul
With gradual language knowing
The caress of boundless heaven

Those giants now walk upon
This short soft grass of evening
Across low oscillating shadow
The yellow and green of light
Quick young swallows in the air
Prepare for their first migration
Like slight ingenious souls who
Are about to quit the living
Oblivious are those footsteps

~ Song Of The Republic ~

As they move out of time
Unaware of the flashing birds
Of endurance and aspiration
The phase of those feet disperses
When night falls on the lawn

Ephemeral and fragile
Are those lives we do not know
They pass about our days
Among the yielding trees
Like those sharp birds who
Have learned how to fly
From casual human distress
Departing in haste and silence
Entering rare altitudes
Undistracted and unseen
Their kindness briefly bends
Touches upon our mortal apex
For no goodwill ever greets
This lawless lightless world

We thought we had long fields
That the land was ours to govern
That bees and grasshoppers and
The small new young swallows
Would live forever in their voice
That our harvest would be endless
Yet as the vessel now inclines
To windward and closely bends
Its carved and feminine head
Toward a diamond where sea and sky
Fuse in one bright dimension
What is it we now proclaim
To secure all moral effort
That virtuosity we pretended

~ Song Of The Republic ~

Who can resist leaves falling
Or stay a wing from flight
In the corridors of promise
No footfall ever walks aside
Smoke rises from the horizon
And like a steely anvil takes
No imprint nor mark as
All our given words dissolve
When great hands reach down
Offering an obscure embrace
And with the golden skin
Which only truth extinguishes
Only then we apprehend
The mastery of life

PIA

When day is sheathed in night
Kestrels and swallows hide
A tall hawk sits waiting
As intruding shadows vanish

The moral beauty of nature
Makes brief issue of her love
Revealing to her devotees
Who like statues observe -

Misery of human solitude
In the face of each day
As the sun comes to mourn
For those who walk alone

Like grief their void shadow
Follows each quiet pace
Going before and after
Even in their sleeping

As wings upon the shoulders
Of a bird departing or
Wheels upon a golden axle
Circling in the future -

So much comes and goes
In such unseen haste
Yet no second is captured
To be held within our hands

Years vanish into sand
So much ingenuity and
Round stones grinding lives
A necklace of experience

~ Song Of The Republic ~

The river of nature runs
Pouring out its slow life -
Human thirst for truth
For pattern in the universe

That water makes us hunger
Floods us with desire
It is not only darkness
But the light of currency -

The great ancestral sky
Where life descends and rises
An oak tree and its bird
Evening of a human day

In the eyes of a statue
Nothing moves or changes
Light passion even death
Is not apparent in those hollows

Only if we transfigure
And our union is revealed
Is there fame within a heart -
Indestructible and clear
For this the hawk awaits

ELLA

The stainless mirror of awareness
Uncreated and so perfect
Cadence of a human pulse
Measuring the universe
Involving earthly time

Silvery and shining like
Fluid that is just alive
Motionless yet implying
All that moves for a while
For light compels us now

Our first freedom was like hay
In a quiet winter barn
Where intimate we held
All that we might need
Caught in summer's odour

The second freedom was in loving
Giving more than we received
The third was in watching
Becoming slow and beautiful
Like a river in the dark

The fourth freedom lay
Embedded in our lust
Inscribed at night by stars
Like moonlight on the snow
When nothing can be said
A vision we concealed

~ Song Of The Republic ~

For no one understood
How long ago in youth
We crossed the fertile sea
Bitter waves of loneliness
Cold in a grey-green flood
Until we reached the rocks -
If we do not comprehend
Human suffering we
Cannot know this world

Between us and the sun
Only time survives
When on a sublime lake
We stared at the hills as
Truth stood on a mountain
Sanguine optimistic
Stripping us of falsehood

We became a girl in heart
A young man in his blood
A lioness walking on a plain
When the world slept

Those were our first rights
And beside a fire we shared
The stones we learned to cut
Where it was simply written
Stars and grass and love
Were only one and conscience
Could not be futile
As hand in hand through days
Our promises were kept

THEA

As the sun enters the lion
Chromium dust filters evening
Time becomes like a dim water
Where we go without saying
Upon a glittering reflective sea

The nerveless unconscious ocean
Where life thinks of nothing
And there is no efficacy -
Where a soul leaves the body
Mourning the memory it deserts

Naked without desire as
It hurtles through night and space
Towards unimaginable islands
Where the sun never settles
And there are only white birds -
Lion of human luminosity
Going lightly among the hours
Beneath the eyelids of long day

EVA

As bees are to pollen so
Are words to a bride
Undressing in darkness
Ancient children of night

Where blood enters blood
Without dust we become
Yet cannot outpace
One just moral pulse

The light which holds us
In its arms caresses
Slow hands disclosing
All life to perception -

In these empty shells
Of successive new days
Where the sky pretends
To know of desolation

In this our freedom
The whetstones of time -
The heroes of beauty
Are perfectly loving

Deer in a dream
Run away too soon
From the warm superhuman
Sweetness of panthers

Or bronze statues falling
Like deities - headless
Worn stones at our feet
Are millennia of years

Song Of The Republic

Now every thin shadow
Is gently withdrawn
As we walk on a thousand
Previous grey hours

Thank you for midnight
Which allowed us to see
For loneliness that made
Us aware of the world

Thank you for anguish
Which gives us the vision
To grasp what is not
Known by a name

This light which bears us
In its weightless hands
So we barely exist -
There is joy in that

Seedless rootless
The source of life is fluent
And the bride and groom
Never rest from loving

~ Song Of The Republic ~

MONA

The ingenuity of the sky
That rules us with schemes
Corn wheat barley and
White dust upon bronze grain

Pleasure of supernal rain
Windows open to the air
Sound of water running down
From eaves to craving earth

Fields bleached by moonlight
Like marble statues in the dark
Owls and foxes hunt the night
Whilst deer feed on wet grass

Sheep are resting on the hills
As pheasant search at dusk
Young horses keep to shadows
Where boys tell stories

Monochrome in the midnight
The woods are still and dry
Timeless and unworldly now
As if poised for ever

Bails of hay are stacked and
Their scent rises slowly
Young men and women find
Themselves so unclothed

What pattern do they create
In their careless loving
Upon the powdery earth and
Its ancient clinging dust

~ SONG OF THE REPUBLIC ~

In the fullness of their passion
The sky above flashing lightly
What impulse of the universe
Is secured in what they hold

DORA

The beauty of a new young moon
Slim candid and so innocent
Like knowledge without belief
Feckless and yet compelling

Tawny bronze and shining
Are the small dry apples
Evening shadows now incline
Long sensuous and satisfied

Sensing a sudden cool air
Trees change their clothing
Prepare to undress quietly
Exposing their limbs

Do you remember that land
Where cyclamen and poppies
Would appear now as the sea
Along the coast became cold

If immortality is the knowing
That we do not exist
Then mariners who set out
Voyaging toward truth -

Approach that strange shore
Within a human heart
Where rays of light are greater
Than the sun of any life

Paths where we once walked
Sometimes sleeping in the groves
Where cicadas proclaimed noon
And dust was perfectly still

~ Song Of The Republic ~

The art of voyaging becomes
Our genius for grief
Knowing what was given as
Undying - without amnesty

The nakedness of young life
And easiness of pleasure
Immutable is the bride
Within these falling hours

We pass through those flames
Purified of our own poor fire
A few embers remain
Hidden among the rocks

Those loves which failed
Which can never be retrieved
Nor resharpened with a spark
Nor invisible knife

We cannot endure a life
Of infidelity where speech
Has no tense and faith
Is stripped of humility

How quickly the sun goes
So fast is human blood
We keep nothing in our arms
Except what time incurs

Worthless yet compelling
Is the need for sweet fruit
The destiny of affection
Or lucid universe revealed

GALA

The beauty of lakes
In their solitude
Covered in shadow
Where kingfishers love

The beauty of rivers
Strong and motive
Whose current is home
When ships return

The beauty of mariners
Who know these things
Unspeakable coasts
Terrain they have touched

Beauty of leaves
Making masts and spars
Ribbed decks of boats
Which journey at sea

How life is displaced
By a bevelled wind
As it draws on a sail
Taking vessels away

True lovers who
Simply know all this
To navigate
Old skies and stars

Black sinuous shoals
Mirror the flashing
Of dry naked clouds
In a vacant sphere

~ Song Of The Republic ~

Where years circle
As cranes now depart
Swallows humming-birds
Even small falcons

Some visit the luminous
Invisible isles
Others tread darkness
So compulsively

This autonomous life
As trees become boats
Or young men and women
Grow silent in time

On impossible paths
Unbetrayed they
Struggle with death
Ordeals to be free

Enjoined by sorrow
To suffer apart
Where courage inwardly
Happily bounds

A voice from the sea
Is calling them home
Ingenuous light
With its cargo of dust

Those who love
The beauty of water
Are never alone
Or among the stars lost

ELENA

The suffering of light is not shadowy
But consciousness of moral dark
Obsidian and elliptical
Yet profound in its dignity
Becoming everything on earth
Possible to apprehension
Even life that gleams beyond the sun

We fail to comprehend the beautiful
In auburn-crimson autumn's slow
Fruition that transforms us from
The fertile and creative
To that black instant before renewal
When we briefly realise how true
Were all the errors and illusion

What rings can marry us to life
In this fugitive death of the year
What circles of conception
Shall bring us to that presence
Of beautifully moving truth
What courage drives a narrow river
Toward a cold grey infinite sea

How wonderful is grief itself
Marking us with empty love
For suffering - light is universal
Completely without pause or rest
We ourselves are those slim shadows
Sheltering beneath obscure trees
As the sun goes to its west

BARBRA

Behold that man that one
Of implacable finesse
Who standing in the wind
In cold stiletto rain
Smiles at our distress

That woman who despite
All the gathering darkness
Where dead leaves are swept
Into the same old river
Only smiles at our enigma

Behold the infant boy or girl
Who dancing barefoot shouts
For the pleasure of a song
Words that have no meaning
Laughing at each minute -

The seconds and the instants
That are tissue and blood
Fluid substance and thread
Of all our unnumbered days
Consumed and justly diminished

Behold how we renew
Naked and mysterious now
For slowness is always beautiful
As the true sun of life
Constantly returns

Behold the fresh devotion
The lover and the young kind
Every small animated being
Creatures who join impassioned
To realise one moment's joy

~ SONG OF THE REPUBLIC ~

We struggle in the vineyard
Among a thousand fallen leaves
To acquire one pure wet taste
Where the world is not deceived
And there is just reception

Snow now unifies the earth
Within a singular perfection
As lovers in their first sweetness
Witness the nerves revealed -
There is nothing like that

Large dark birds are waiting
Blue and rouge in the trees
Stepping quietly through the grass
They stare at us in silence
Waiting for our breath to pause

For this is all we know
The seed in the grain and
The water in the sky falling
Wind passing across our face
As the universe says repeatedly
Behold the only promise

LYDIA

UNDER thin metal oak leaves
Vibrating in frozen west wind
Deer and owls are collecting
Foxes come to sniff at bones
Under a pink and apricot dawn

A hawk strips a poor meal
A rabbit limps for want of grass
Crows are silenced by the cold
Cross a bare cerulean sky
Above the mineral oak leaves

Whose the grey bones the hair
Whose the slow starvation
Did anyone desire that body once
When it was gold and heated

LILIA

THE first thin snow silences
A world with its evening
Small birds grow quiet as
Shadows seep to the earth

A colourless sky descends
With slow circular mystery
As cold watery vapour
Gathers about points of life

Unspeakably lone and separate
We await an ideal birth
A young and avid new light
With all goodness of kind

In their nakedness the trees
Move slightly in desperation
Coldness enters into stone
The river struggles with darkness

Pheasant woodcock and quail
Eyes closed with hunger
Hide carefully amid the stubble
Fox and rabbit halt and wait

Fields remain untouched now
Deer tread vigilant in search
Of rare grass and sustaining moss
To sleep among damp reeds

~ Song Of The Republic ~

We pause in our oblivion
Surrendering to solitude
Where milky radiance hovers
Urging us toward a fire

If consciousness is apart
From this sensible world
That experience is our truth
Origin of living amity

What ancient feet now walk
On raw granite hills
What features of the universe
Oversee our dubiety -

Ribbons of experience and
Fabric of all sensation
A nucleus of certain union
Joining creatures in their rest

This one true cell in which
We first become aware
Like an undefended child
Staring at an icy world

The frail snow censors
Human ignition and suffering
As shadows justly promise
Intimacy and affection

SARA

INITIATIVE of light and birds
Passing through a gateway
Hills draw ancient darkness
Where fidelity vibrates

We are wreathed in coldness
Enclosed by damp earth
The cadence of lovers
Is hidden among leaves

When you love do not
Let it fly from your hands
Regardless of misery
Or its cause of despair

Like the keel of a boat
Or an autumn plough
Copper nails rusting and
Oars so abandoned -

This boat has wings and
Its torn crimson hull
Has two black eyes
That are always famished

If you love then all
The world is observed
However solitary
Your excluded hours

If you love you receive
Just one gift of vision
To be always a witness
Of what no one knows

~ Song Of The Republic ~

Through mineral gates
Our life shall depart
Stripped of lightness
As if shot from a bow

Like the mystery of music
Yet no anthem is heard
An incendiary predator
Who calls out in time

As boats have their vision
Pursue lonely courses
Without oblivion
Is this human archery

Despite our removal
Grainy dust of years
What you love becomes
More perfect than kind

Hovering in silence
And lightly inspected
We are simply weighed
As we pass like birds

You are the lover and
No one is apart
For loving has joined you
Outside of this world

If the aim is life
And the end is true
There is no death
Given your promise

NINA

I AM silenced by your beauty
Fluent light of your eyes
Stainless immoveable and lovely
Is your unbreakable desire

The misery that you inspired
And resentment cultivated
All these like summer rain
Could not overwhelm the fountain

In love with the unbetrothed
You turned into stone
And thinking of your freedom
You only became impulsive

Now you age beyond life
And at evening recall
So much reckless dalliance
Nothing can make you smile

Yet your beauty makes me quiet
There is water in your laughter
Even the garments you wear
Still imply your loveliness

What is to be said at last
There are flaws in our vision
Should slaves become impassioned
By what they never possess

BEATRICIA

I THOUGHT my grief would never end
That my solitude would fill the world
And I would die of weeping
That no one on earth would know

Like wild grass that falls and dies
Without the warmth of summer rain
So I thought my time was finished
When you went away this morning

Love can travel a thousand miles
In less than one second
And when we die all that remains
Is life – that is what they say

In the engine-room of the heart
There always is a sound of beating
Even if there is no wind
Sails move back and forth

Since your departure I
Am subtracted by futility
There remains no happiness
In any second any more

So I have lightly climbed
This invisible iron stair
For so many years alone
Without companion voice

This solitary grey ascent
Where even swallows and hawks
Have departed from these skies
Of quickly changing colour

~ Song Of The Republic ~

The wind runs round about
Circling spherical days
What is there now to see
And - must we still arise

Even though our eyes close
There remains so much
Irresolution to this sadness
Solitude without horizon

Without you I am vacant
Dry motionless and untouched
Without your wild sea-mood of blood
This world becomes so speechless

VITA

The absent forms of beauty
That like unseen figures guide
Our steps and slow inclination
Where all our imperfection
Moves with random time
Not deflected as a sudden light
Is caught upon a piece of glass
Or dashed upward from a lake
Or transient river where the water
Goes quicker than a blade
The compassion of those rare beings
Makes us more than we are
Leading us through passing moments
Where truthfulness is kindness

Now apples acorns passage birds
Vehement lovers in the fields
All purpose in the universe
Endeavor and exertion
Survive by chancing darkness
To learn of coldness in the world
Like modest deer among tall stones
Or hawks visiting on tree-tops
Or friendship that always loves
More than passion can
This mystery of suffering when
The declining hours retract
And trees expose their wealth
Telling of the unspeakable

Now furrows are inscribed
Like sufficient words directing
The underworld to reform us
So we might find bearing
Union which a compass knows
The optimistic metal needle

~ Song Of The Republic ~

And shivering of direction
Like fluent syllables on tongues
Which score our humanity
The instruments of this life
Are not those of love but
The fidelity of what we say
And senseless we forgo the sun
With an unmoved archery

Now lonely ships set off from port
Animated by low setting planets
Where north becomes reversed
And the pleasing nakedness
Of amorous unclothed couples
Who sleep upon a mutable shore
Surrounded by old promises
Is lost and irreversibly forgotten
Like kingfishers in temporal light
Where the unbreakable is still
A curving world redressing life
Or the impermanently beautiful
That catches us with tissue breath
Reviving our perpetual freedom

SERENA

EARLY morning like a shepherd
Through dense grey light
Going by fields and rivers
Protecting immortality from time

Where we wait for the wind
In a silent trickling air
As cold thin arid rain
Drives away human radiance

If the mystery of suffering
Is this perfect challenge
The secrecy of courage
Becomes our call or demand

It is so dark and the sun
Just touches our blood
Taking us from life toward
That long moral arch

Where the sun steps forward
Barefoot onto wet grass
Like friendship – the day
Revives us with its eyes

So what was all that loving
Such tense intoxication
Were those companions truly
Patient in their honesty

When the armour of speech
Shone like refracted fire
And the visor of affection
Covered our weak parts

~ Song Of The Republic ~

Was there an ardent cause
Blue moment when a cry
Emptied the world of solitude
In that first early morning

Early morning as the night
And its darkness decease
When the origin of our kind
And fragrance is hidden

What might we conceive
As we fall asleep at last
What image like a hawk
Passes before our vision

Early morning as we stare
At friends who approach
Saluting from the shadow
Calling us to join their pace -

Upon a small white boat
That stills its sails a moment
Waiting for us to board
To set off one more time

On a fertile glittering sea
Without sky or horizon
Translucent and untouchable
In its unspeakable ways

That traceless new voyage
Where insensible at last
Our conscious body is
Weightless and without pain

JULIA

On the knife edge of the year
Invisible point where we exchange
Casually waiting until we are
Lightly given away in time

Where silver birds pass quickly
High fast and moving like
Small shining glittering lives
As if seeds of a new kind

Faster than time itself they
Cross an altitude of light
Above a curving blameless sky
Dashing as they vanish

Like a sound of bells in darkness
Quicker than stars or dust they
Go passing slightly above earth
Realising future goodness

We close our eyes to the small
Narrow hours of a concave day
As the year collapses and then
Reveals anew a lucid world

Despite so much cold dark rain
All of life is so reformed
The gravity of dense heaven
Disdains human loneliness

What season lives within this sight
Autumn or summer upon a loom
Where affection has no surplus
And there is no destination

~ SONG OF THE REPUBLIC ~

We saw the ardent grain buried
One morning before dawn
With the treaty of another age
Where suffering was not spoken

KARINA

BRING some water it is time
To drink to swear our end
Run the boat towards the edge
Now we must go home

Fetch white oars from racks
Embrace old friends and take
The hard-wood tiller from
Above the hearth - bring grain
For the advancing future

Soon ice will sheathe our blades
Then thirst will make us dumb
Wounds will refuse to join
Lips be sore and hardened
Now we have said everything

Leave behind the torn charts
We know the sun's routine
We have our own metaphors
We breathe - a laughless sea
The shell of night awaits

White canvas covers the hull
Stiff upon frames and ribs
A lack of gravity keeps us
From falling onto rocks
For we have nothing to lose

Bring water let us drink
Unclothed and undisguised
We only wear a visor now
Our souls are made of water
Lift the hull toward the edge

~ Song Of The Republic ~

When the sun a milky spot
In the sky and we unseen
Stripped of all but memory
Then we truly live - stayed
By lucid friendship

Ospreys will follow diving
Into our wake for fish
Petrels shall build their nest
In foam left by our stem
Dolphins bring us to sleep

The glare of a true sun
Will cleanse our icy purpose
Saline green of swell will teach
Us to repeat - initial words
We once learned to say

We are the first ship and
Sea-deities will amaze to see
Us crossing above - they
Who thought they were alone
Potent undenied till now

Sea-weed sea-gull gleaming
Sand-bank flats where rivers
Fuse their current in the draw
And withdrawal of salt tide
Low stony isles of pine forest

A few rough spars beached
Will be all that ever remains
To sing of us and tell
How we vanished from life
Disappeared from a world

~ Song Of The Republic ~

Printed by dustless forms
Our songs are whiter than
Marble or breaking wave
Stronger than brass or iron
Letters pressed in granite base

Neither rain nor rust nor
Death's liberty nor melting
Fire can touch them now
We have gone home where
None but friendship counts

Thinking we never end
Between houses we left
And islands recalled there
Is only pretence of dignity
Trials of kindness - say

Like a bottle of water
Dropped into an ocean
Sinking before it breaks
Like a pebble of salt
Dissolved in the sea
Fusing in cold waves

In our adventures
We are consumed
Vanish into the rest
As glass shatters and
Water mixes with ocean
We become all that we were

AMARA

WHAT is the grain of these days
What vessel can we build
And store its hold for years
Of long and solitary voyage

Who knows what passages
Await us and what horizon
We might possibly exceed
Vanishing from known existence

So build yourself a firm ship
That shall never founder
Made of wind and trees and iron
For every course of happiness

Make a compass out of love
A hull bound with affection
Giving more than it receives
To all the passing waves

May the fragrance of the ocean
Archery of a starry heaven
Drive the ship through all its years
Until we forget our name

May your companions be like birds
With their secret midnight music
And may all the shadowy fish
Keep your course away from rocks

Place hard stones upon your keel
To remind you of the misery
That you put aside when leaving
Port and all that old grief

~ Song Of The Republic ~

For that will bring you gravity
Shall keep your boat upright
Despite sharp gales that torment
When no breeze moves your heart

Then one day when that white isle
Appears to be before your eyes
As anchors fall and sails collapse
And you are free of ordeal

On that shore of happiness
There is no print upon the sand
There is no one and no body
Where you lie down and rest

~ Song Of The Republic ~

DOMNA

There are two cities on earth
Divided by time and kindness
And at the centre of their field
Is a king who sits in silence

About him move the reapers
Drawing in the living grain
Goodness or the void deceit
That human life advances

On the edges of this world
Just beyond the known blue rim
Are mortal doubt and anxiety
Glittering with so much disbelief

In one city there is despair
Meaningless desolation
Where sickles of severe abuse
Cut and harvest emptiness

Sometimes moral predators
Destroy us in the night
When ambushed by cruelty
We are wrecked by extreme contempt

In another city there is judgement
Where a palpable soul is weighed
And the words our tongues exchange
Are assessed for generosity

Beyond the urban walls there is
A worn green altar on a plain
Where smoke is offered to the sky
And blood poured on the stones

~ Song Of The Republic ~

There are the unwritten stars
Calculating every hour
Few who walk this level world
Observe their silence and precision

There are brides grooms and lovers
Where the youthful go apart
To meet indelibly and completely
Offering all they might possess

There are songs of the universe
That recall for us a truth
Words forsaken in our effort
When we only pursue ourselves

There are small lakes and rivers
Running down toward a coast
And on the hills are quick hawks
Who play upon a thin grey wind

There are vineyards and groves
And orchards where boys and girls
Laugh among the grassy shadow
Lightly clothed with future promise

Just like a dancing floor all this
Was prepared without a single wound
Perfectly beautiful and still
Where years are made immobile

Although we see the movement
Are impelled by human currency
Yet nothing happens or can change
In the eyes of this ardent king

ZORA

The genius of a bird at dawn
Singing in warm darkness
Of how to touch someone
If there is no one there

For nothing is postponed
There is only one instant
Uniquely recurring and
Driving our tidal blood

Yet in what channel does
Destiny secure this life
What currency is conveyed
If the sky is benign

Just as the stars dance
Upon our heads in sleep
More than light we are
Secret in our piety

Every stone and callous rock
Is noosed by the same humility
That sprays our desire
When happiness is impressed

So too the confluence of time
Captures us in haste
Yet we believe that being driven
Is a knowledge we can hold

Then a little wooden boat
Without an anchor comes
A voice calls out - saying
Step quickly for this is all
The sovereignty you might obtain

~ Song Of The Republic ~

We are only what we received
When all the bones were tossed
Into the cold night air as
Our conception was composed -
A rumour once devised in blood

Now we are soaked
Like hawks in light and wind
Above the lake pines sand
As grasses bend and susurrate

For destiny is always guarded
Hidden from us by quietness
And what is most unbearable
Is our own lack of courage

Shall we ever be free or
Does light simply weigh us
So we might only descend
Like a bright hawk stooping

When all the topaz beauty
Of the world as we know it
All loveliness and its clouds
All turn to carbon shadow

Vicissitude affection
Horror at human loneliness
Are hidden in the eye of a bird
In the sound of that voice

What shall we say when
There is no further ritual
When the ancestors we admired
Retreat to the mountains
To stare at us in silence

~ Song Of The Republic ~

Men and women stray no more
As hawks strike at swallows
Rooms remain closed and
Children are unheard in
Dry dusty and autumnal truth

Birches and cedars sway in hours
Above a stony rock shelf
Sails pass in the distance going
Far out across the lake
Waves of water fill the night

Two hawks come down the air
Finding home among the pines
They bring us recollection
Of how life once endured
When the sky was observed

In ceremonies of daylight
Destruction and creation
Where each consumes another
The immanent is fulfilled so
We become more transparent

Up and down the light we go
As upon a hidden stair
Giving all we can whilst
Time is in our hands then
Surrendering to the play of birds

~ Song Of The Republic ~

Who in their night-journeys
Are moved by the glare
Of a glassy shining beacon
As hawks poise and wait upon
The rails of a lighthouse
Keen to tear the breast
To draw out the brain
Of all attracted swallows

Swallows long to travel
Just as hawks choose to kill
This fusion of experience
And of certain knowledge
Brings about a mutual death
Union of voyage and terminus
Of flyer talon and breathing

Without swallows hawks are vague
Without the beacon swallows
Never realise the truth of how
Distance and imperative in life
Do not convey the honesty
Of flight and its memorable end -
The swallow delivers to the hawk
This rite of consciousness

Our understanding of the world
Is converted by each step
We make as we daily glide
And walk into a bare future
Making human wakefulness
All that we cannot know -
How our end is more than light

~ Song Of The Republic ~

Now we decline to darkness
Eternal condition of the universe
Of all life and disposition
Obscurity that bears us

Days become warmer richer
Yet they are lessened now
Diminished and reduced by
An increasing ring of shade

Rounded by all we do or say
As the horizon contracts
Where only friendship tells
Of goodness and its worth

As a procession painted
Upon a hanging cloth
We are like a circle of kings
Appearing to move and respire

A slight motion of the air
Causes the pattern to quiver
Yet nothing ever occurs
And no word is spoken

The red-haired boys and girls
Whose attraction is unearthly
About their feet the sun dances
Passing invisible gates

So we admire firm beauty
Which only we perceive
Observing compassion in
The hands of human amity

~ Song Of The Republic ~

More than earthly nature
More than blood or breath
Momentarily fixed we are
Changed and so transcend

Now as the season fails
Falling from perfect zenith
How to make life reflare
To out-brighten this one day

Ordeals only make us brave
With gratitude for kindness
We are not devoured now
Become even more ravenous

All the ships we have known
Islands songs music houses
All the landscape and people
All recede and desist

Soon lakes rivers seas
Shall grow cooler - warmth less
As small birds vanish with
Migration and annual decease

Yet our words shall stay a little
Longer in time and vision
Before they too discover how
Wonderful are dust and shadow

The light of early morning
Sends its shearing edge forward
Sacrificing with red blades
The grey creation of this world

~ SONG OF THE REPUBLIC ~

Like wild grass that bends and dies
An instrument of days we are
Nucleus of the universe
Whose rings we cannot touch

~ Song Of The Republic ~

THERE is a ring that lovers wear
Made of light and transparent stone
That weightless cannot be destroyed
Nor can it be exchanged

Like a shallow dish of shining water
That might never be withheld
Or those perfect figures who approach
To hover in our solitude

This ring joins us in the world
Away from living human time
And when we drink of this love
Suffering is stripped and falls

There is nothing else on earth
No vessel moving through the days
For once we accept this round
There is no possible rest

AFTERWORD

AMERICAN WOMEN are unlike the women of other continents in that their relations to hierarchy, convention, and social dimension are uniquely different. For instance, in the speeches of Susan Anthony, in the character of Laura Ingalls Wilder, in the pictures of women that were made in the Thirties by Dorothea Lange, even in the words of Eleanor Roosevelt, a new kind of femininity can be witnessed. These figures are akin to the women of Homeric Odyssey where the journey homeward of the hero is actually facilitated and enabled by the conversations which he experiences with various feminine kinds: they are the ones who conduce to his return towards kingdom.

Modern feminism is a manner that is primarily and historically American in origin and in this the place of the *femme fatale* can be considered as a philosophical ideal, an hypothesis that allows us close readers of the past and of literature to apprehend an iconic model of femininity. By *femme fatale* I would indicate a pure form of human consciousness that—due to its clarity and natural authenticity—is without critical volition and is wholly respondent and only receptive: it completely transcends its own material self. This is an archaic form of what we might consider as the *feminine* and I would assert that such heroic autonomy always reflects how best to move, for that is the ground of a truly subtle agency which knows how to become discrete. In a structural and non-durable sense this is the primary ancient *psyche*.

Consciousness is not something which humans are born with but it is received—like language, cultural valence, or emotion—and these forces formulate how it is that we consider ourselves as becoming aware: it is the feminine which makes this work initially creative of all possible human worth.

What I have depicted in the poetry contained within these pages represents that original sentience or understanding, one which can be said to be *nature without instinct*. The myth of the American Woman is founded upon such autochthonous tendencies. Nowadays, as human liberty becomes excessively exposed this exceptional condition is rarely to be possessed in that it only passes through us and resides beyond all time, briefly inhabiting our terrestrial character.

Kevin M<small>C</small>G<small>RATH</small> was born in southern
China in 1951 and was educated in
England and Scotland; he has lived and worked
in France, Greece, and India. Presently he is
an Associate of the Department of South Asian Studies
and Poet Laureate at Lowell House, Harvard University.
Publications include, *Fame* (1995), *Lioness* (1998),
The Sanskrit Hero (2004), *Flyer* (2005), *Comedia* (2008),
Stri (2009), *Jaya* (2011), *Supernature* (2012),
Eroica, and *Heroic Krsna* (2013), *In the Kacch* and
Windward (2015), *Arjuna Pandava* and *Eros* (2016),
Raja Yudhisthira (2017, *Bhisma Devavrata* (2018),
Vyasa Redux (2019), and *On Friendship* (forthcoming, 2021).
McGrath lives in Cambridge, Massachusetts,
with his family.

www.ingramcontent.com/pod-product-compliance
Lightning Source LLC
Chambersburg PA
CBHW032232080426
42735CB00008B/825